NANCY YOUNTZ SHEFF
BIG MAMA NANCY'S

Advice

ACKNOWLEDGEMENTS

I would like to first of all, thank my Lord, and Savior Jesus Christ for loving me and dying for me. God is everything to me. Then I want to thank my beautiful daughter Victoria, and my wonderful granddaughter's Madison, Kennedy and Courtland, who give me unconditional love and support. I thank my adoptive parents Veroble and Clara Yountz for taking me in when I had no place to go and for instilling good values in me. I want to thank my grandmother by birth, the late Gladys Wilson, who was without doubt the strongest woman I have ever met. She taught me that while it would be great to have a good man, the fact that you don't have one is no excuse for pursuing your dreams and being successful. I want to thank my spiritual mother, Nancy Hunter, for her never-ending prayers and support through the years. And a heart-felt thanks to all my family who stood by me through the years.

And a special thanks to Veronica Vale Upchurch for the beautiful cover photo

FOREWORD

Life is a maze that we all have to navigate and find our way through. It is full of many decisions as to which way we can turn. These turns take us through success, fulfillment and happiness or failures, disappointments and regrets. How do we make the right choices to prevent us from traveling down the wrong road that leads to despair? In this highly engaging but short dissertation, Nancy Yountz-Sheff offers relevant, timely, and helpful answers.

Nancy focuses in razor-sharp fashion on key areas of life and suggests life lessons learned by attending the school of "Hard Knocks," working in private nursing car facilities, and sitting at the feet of her grandmother. Being diagnosed with clinical depression and later attaining victory over it, Nancy knows firsthand what it takes to gain access to a healthy path and to continue one's journey without looking back. Because of her now optimistic and hopeful outlook, shared in an intimate and heartfelt prose, Nancy diligently chronicles a proven way forward.

Unfortunately, there are far too many people, young and old, rich and poor, male and female, who have chosen the wrong road and now stand at the crossroads of a decision, wondering which way to go. This book provides a useful road map and guide to assist a reader in their decision-making and enhance their destiny.

As a fellow navigator, I would like to applaud and celebrate Nancy for writing this thought-provoking and discerning book. Reading the manuscript made me realize that I am a beneficiary of Big Mamma Nancy's advice and by walking down the road ascribed in this book, I too can say I am a better person, husband, father, and friend.

—JAMES R. GORHAM
Brigadier General (Retired)
United States Army
Author of *Sharecropper's Wisdom*

1. Stop looking for someone to make you happy and complete. You must take the time to focus on yourself and let Jesus heal you, and find your sufficiency in Him and not look to others. Learn to be happy alone and enjoy your own company before you meet someone, and when the right person comes along, they will enjoy your company as well.

2. Contrary to common belief, there are good single men and women out there. They may be hard to find but they are out there. I know this because I am one of them. Some are disguised by the defensiveness and overprotection of their heart because of past pain, but they are out there. If you meet someone that you really like, think of them like Shrek. Shrek said that he is like an onion, with many layers. If they are good at their core, with a good heart and good values, take the time to peel back the layers. No one is perfect. We are all a work-in-progress. Find someone that you like and care for and put in the work to develop a good relationship as you continue your journey of self-discovery and self-development. Be patient and develop trust, respect, and appreciation. These are the foundations of a healthy relationship.

3. Always treat your significant other with respect and appreciation. Never take them for granted. Let them know that you value them and want them in your life. Out of all the people in the world they chose to be with you. Don't make them regret it. Treat them like a queen or a king. Don't be afraid to throw rose petals at their feet like royalty. In the Bible, Sarah honored Abraham and called him Lord. Don't choose to be with anyone that you can't trust and respect.

4. Love is very important in a relationship but it is not all-important or paramount. Many people love someone, or think they do, but they cannot trust them and don't respect them. That kind of so-called love will only bring you pain. Love is not supposed to hurt. Read 1 Corinthians 13. It is called the "Love Chapter." It tells you what true love is and does. Love will uplift you and make you want to do and be better. Love brings you together. It doesn't push you apart. Don't misunderstand. No one and no relationship is perfect. But if loving them is destroying you, then it is not love at all.

5. This statement is not mine, but it is true. "You can catch more flies with honey than with vinegar." That is true in any relationship. Both casual and intimate relationships. You must learn how to talk to people. The Bible

says that "A soft answer turns away wrath." Proverbs 15:1. Learn how to speak softly. Sweeten your tone and don't be abrasive. Don't use hurtful words that pierce the heart and soul. The old saying that 'sticks and stones may break my bones, but words will never hurt me' is a lie. Words can hurt you very deeply and once those words are released they can't be taken back. And those piercing wounds don't heal quickly. Work on developing effective communication. The mirroring technique is a very good method to use to limit misunderstandings. When you say something to your partner or child, have them repeat it back to you, so that you both have a clear understanding of what is expected.

6. When it comes to sex, make sure that you are on the same page and compatible. Sex should be discussed before marriage. You need to know what each of you feels is important, and what you can and cannot go without. Frequency should also be discussed. This will save you both a lot of frustration in the future and will be a good indicator of whether or not the relationship will last or if infidelity may be a problem that you face in the future.

7. True love is worth waiting for and working towards. It is priceless and worth more than gold. If you both want

the relationship, take your time, and put in the work to develop a strong one with a solid foundation that will stand the test of time. Work on the front-end and make the job of maintaining the relationship in the future easy. It is not easy to start a fire but keeping the fire going is not hard. Don't let the fire go out, you will have to work to start it again. If you both want the relationship, because it takes two to tango. Make the investment in each other and the relationship. Do the work. Love hard. Respect and appreciate each other. Communicate effectively and protect what you have built. Create a love-affair that will last a life-time. It can be done. I have been with my sweetheart almost seven years and it just keeps getting better. As a woman who loves extremely hard and passionately, I have put in most of the work. Because I see and saw something in him that even he did not see. I was patient, and I loved, nurtured, and encouraged him through difficult times. And I am so glad I did.

8. Don't ever stop praising God. My profession of faith is that the name of the Lord is worthy to be praised. No matter what happens, the name of the Lord is still worthy to be praised. I also continually state that God is sovereign, and all His ways are right. I trust Him completely because He is sovereign and all His ways are

right. When I don't understand, He is sovereign and all His ways are right. Never stop trusting and praising God.

9. I Thessalonians 5:15 Don't give evil for evil but follow that which is good. Just because someone says or does something against you doesn't mean that you have to do the same. Vengence is mine, I will repay says the Lord. Romans 12:19. The Lord will fight your enemies and give you the victory. Deuteronomy 20:4. God will make your enemies your footstool. Psalm 110:1. You never need to fight people. Don't lower yourself to their level. Many people are extremely petty and immature. Don't be like them. One of my favorite quotes is by Michelle Obama. She says "when they go low, we go high." That is the best attitude to have when dealing with people. Rise above them and their mess. Don't get involved. Take the high road. Respect yourself and be dignified. In time, the truth will come out. Hold your peace. Keep quiet. And in time, God himself will vindicate you. You don't need to dirty yourself by playing in the gutter with trash. Selah (meditate on this).

10. I Corinthians 13-The Love Chapter. Do your best to walk in love with everyone you meet. Some people make this hard to do. But love them as God loves you

even if you must do it from a distance. You can't allow just any and every one close to you. Some people get a sick thrill from hurting people. Some people prey on who they think are weaker people. Have no fear. God will take care of them in time. Some people prey on the innocent, especially children. Matthew 18:6 says that it is better that a millstone be hung around your neck and that you were cast into the sea than to hurt one of God's little ones. That goes for child abusers and molesters. They are sick excuses for human beings getting a thrill from preying on the weak. But rest assured, they will get what is coming to them in one way or another. Prosecute them if possible and put a stop to the abuse, and go on. Let Jesus heal your broken heart and go on with your life. You can live and love freely after abuse. Ask Jesus to help you. He is a miracle-worker.

11. John 3:16 "For God so loved the world that he gave his only son. That whosoever believes in Him should not perish but have eternal life." This is true for everyone, including gay people. Don't make the mistake of thinking that because a person is gay, they are a molester. Child molesters are a special sick, twisted kind of evil. To force themselves on someone who can't fight back is beyond pathetic. Those type of people will never pick a fight with anyone their own size or who is

competition. Gay people, don't let anyone tell you that God doesn't love you. God loves everyone because God is love. I John 4 That doesn't mean that he won't judge those who abuse others. God loved us so much that before we accepted Him He sent His only Son to die for us. God loves us all. But he doesn't like all the things that we do. Selah.

12. Hebrews 11-The Hall Of Faith. Many people believe that the thing that will get their prayers answered is crying, pleading, begging, and moaning. While God is very merciful and doesn't want His children broken hearted, the number one way to get your prayers answered is by real, strong, authentic faith. You must accept Him as your savior according to Romans 10:9-10 then take the time to develop a relationship with Him as your savior and Lord. You can talk to God like you talk to your best friend, speak openly and honestly. There is no need to lie to Him because He sees and knows all. He knows your thoughts before they form in your head. You can't trick or fool Him. Be honest about the way you feel. He already knows. Even though you can't see him, He is there. You can't see the wind either but you know that it is real. He is always with you. Hebrews 13:5 says that He will never leave or forsake you. God is real. God is alive. And God still works

miracles. Matthew 13:58 says that God could do no mighty miracles in a certain city because of their unbelief. You must develop real faith and trust in God to see Him move. No matter what it looks like or feels like, you must walk by faith, not by sight. 2Corinthians 5:7

13. When building that special relationship, be sure to show forth as much love, honor, and respect as possible. Be gentle, kind, and loving. Building a healthy relationship means building the other person up in the same way that you are to build yourself up. Speak well of yourself and them. Esteem others higher than you esteem yourself. Never lose yourself in another person because you are valuable. Simply be the best you and give your best to that special person.

14. Remember to always let people know that they are important to you and that you care for them. Give them flowers while they are living so that you both can enjoy them. Tell and show them that you love them. That way if something bad happens you won't have any regrets about the way that you treated them. Be loving, gentle, and kind. Live a life as free of regret as possible. Live your best life and love fiercely.

15. Never take the people in your life for granted that you love and who loves you. Those who want only the best for you. Those who encourage and pray for you. I have heard it said that you are fortunate if you have two or three real, true friends in your lifetime. Most people don't have that many. I have found that to be true myself. It amazes me how quickly people will betray you and stab you in the back. They will sell you out for nothing. Never allow anyone close to you who does not mean you good and have your best interest at heart. Never allow anyone to abuse or demean you. Love doesn't hurt. Be very careful who you allow in your inner circle. Be sure to love and appreciate those special people that God places in your life. I have a prayer for myself. "God, I thank you for every open door and for every closed door. And thank you for keeping bad people away from me." I carry myself in a friendly, no-nonsense way. And I let people know that I am, as an ex co-worker said "BS intolerant." I have no problem putting anyone in their place, if necessary. And I can do it with a smile. It's a very valuable skill.

16. Please don't adopt a keep up with the Jones attitude. The Jones are in serious debt and are robbing Peter to pay Paul! They are paying their bills with credit cards, then struggling to pay the minimum balance to keep them

open. Then they tell their kids to tell the bill collectors that they are not home when they make the mistake of answering the phone before they check the caller ID. They don't open any mail that looks like a bill and burn it if they do. They are praying one prayer. "Lord please let Publisher's Clearinghouse or the lottery save me." The idea of working hard to pay their way out of the hole they have dug for themselves is foreign. How can a Jones be seen on a part-time job? How would it look if they downsized and get a handle on their finances? People would talk about them and no one living such a shallow life can stand to be talked about. That would ruin the fake image that they have created of their prosperity. It's a ridiculous way to live. As I always say, "you do what you have to do until you can afford to do what you want to do." You work. And have a good work ethic while thanking God that you have a job and the strength to get up and go to work. Be proud of yourself and respect yourself for doing an honest day's work on a legal job. If you want something in life, go after it and work for it. You may have to start at the bottom and work your way up, but do it! You may have to work two or even three jobs at once, but do it! You may have to go to night school, but do it! You may have to work for someone else doing something you don't like to do until you can start your own business and make it profitable, but do it! There is no dishonor in working a job while pursuing your dream. Do what you must on your journey to success. There is no excuse. No valid reason for you not going after what you want in life. But along the way there are bills to pay and mouths to feed. Be a responsible adult and go for it!

17. In 1945, during the World War II, the United States dropped an atomic bomb on Hiroshima and Nagasaki in response to Japan's attack on Pearl Harbor. The atomic blasts virtually destroyed the cities entirely. Then 27 days after the bombing, a tropical storm hit the area. While a tropical storm is not usually a good thing, this tropical storm was because it washed away the radioactivity left by the atomic blast. The tropical storm was named Ann, which in Japanese means "grace." Obviously after the horrendous tragedy of the bombing, the Japanese people recognized how gracious God was to them to allow the storm to help in the healing process. Without the storm the radioactivity would have lingered. Radioactivity can harm the whole body. This is called somatic damage. It can also harm the sperm and eggs which is called genetic damage. Tropical storm Ann helped to minimize this damage to the Japanese people. Why am I giving this history lesson? I assure you that I have a valid point. There is always a method

to my madness. My point is this. As a black female in my 50s who has had many bad things happen in my life which were beyond my control, I don't make excuses or let them stop me from achieving my goals and reaching my happily-ever-after. It pains my heart deeply to hear anyone, especially black people, make excuses for under-achieving as if someone owes them something. "If God be for me He is more than the whole world against me." Romans 8:31. If that is true (and it is), why would you think that the "white man" or any man can hold you down? Why do you buy into the myth of the "glass ceiling"? God has paved the streets of heaven with gold! Is the glass that you, not God, has placed above you stronger than the gold beneath His feet? Glass breaks under pressure. Gold is refined and becomes purer and stronger under pressure. Who do you believe is stronger, God or man? Stop making excuses because there is no excuse. No one can stop you, but you. The white man is not your enemy. You are your own worst enemy if you have that kind of small-minded thinking. God speaks and worlds are formed. The winds and the waves must obey Him, Jesus died and rose to give you abundant life.

NEWSFLASH! It is highly unlikely that you are ever going to receive reparations. Stop looking for and asking for them. I hear people say, "it will happen if it's meant to be". Go make you own meant-to-be! It's your life and it's the only one that you are going to have. Make it count! I pray that you had good parents who didn't hurt, abuse, or molest you and didn't allow anyone else to either. But whether you did or not is not paramount or most important anymore. As an adult you must take control of and be responsible for your own life. Seek the help you need, both legally and through therapy and medicine. If you are having mental and emotional problems stemming from abuse or molestation there are medications that can help. There is no shame in seeking help for yourself and your loved ones. It is this false sense of shame that aids in the continuation of the abuse. The "we don't talk about what goes on in this house" attitude has helped to perpetuate such dis-function for generations. And it is the twisted excuse that perverts use to keep you silent. Mental illness is very prevalent in society and many times families call the person crazy and abandon them instead of assisting in getting them the help they need. That's why there is an opioid epidemic and rampant homelessness. Many people act like if they pretend it isn't happening then it is not real or it will go away. They do this while real people, especially children, are being used and abused for some pervert's sick thrills. We need to help each other, and charity starts at home. Hiroshima was destroyed but was rebuilt in approximately 20 years because of the relentless nature, attitude, and ambition of the Japanese people. They have a "never say die" attitude. They didn't tell future generations that they were at a disadvantage because the Americans destroyed their city and killed their people. They worked harder and now they excel. We can learn a lot from them. As a mature black grandmother, I look at my people and it breaks my heart. The way that our families are fragmented and broken. Women continually having babies by men who care nothing for them or their children. Leaving those children in situations where they are not safe because they have to work to keep their household going while that man is off to the next woman to do the same thing to her and her children. Men so irresponsible, immature, and self-absorbed that they are not looking to take care of anyone, not even themselves. They are looking for a desperate women so needy for attention that she will support him and place herself and her children at risk. The plight of the male is serious, but the plight of the black male is especially of great concern. The way a man can drop his seed in anyone and walk away not caring if the woman he impregnated or the child eats or has a roof over their heads and is much less concerned if they have anything they need and want to make them have a happy life and a chance at a better future than he had. The fact that our families were torn apart during slavery should make us want to build strong, loving families and give the next generation a head start at having a better life. There is no excuse. First, let me say that birth control works for most people if you use it. Please stop getting pregnant before you have built a strong family dynamic to bring the child into, and have gained some degree of financial stability. And please stop getting pregnant to keep these men who don't want to be with you. These children are not glue to hold your family together or hold a man hostage. That is not their responsibility. They didn't ask to come here. Be a good woman and if he doesn't want you, let him leave without being tied to him with a child that he will not likely support financially or emotionally. Even if you can force him to pay child support, that doesn't mean that he will be there for the child and be an active part of his/her life. If you meet a man who has kids and he is not active in their life, the last thing you want to do is have a baby by him. No man who can abandon his children is worth having. That's his innocent child. And if he doesn't care if they are fed, clothed, and have a roof over their head, why would you want him? Don't you know that he will do the same to you and yours. And please stop arguing with and fighting over men who are simply laughing at and playing you both for a fool. Have some dignity and respect for yourself. It is that type of thing that has our race in the condition that it is in. And sadly, when someone decides to better themselves and be responsible, the crab theory kicks in and other black people try to pull them down instead of trying to lift them up. Don't be a hater. So many people are marching the streets yelling "black lives matter". Black lives must first matter to black people before they will matter to any other race. We must stop trying to keep each other down and killing each other. We can start now to work together and build a new era of positive people who help each other and support each other. And create a race that we can truly brag about in a positive way for the positive things that we have done.

18. Effective communication is very important in all facets of life but it is especially important in your close personal relationships with family and friends. Let the people that you care about know how you feel and make sure that they are safe and secure in your love and concern for them. Never let them question or doubt how you feel about them. If they died today, would you have guilt or regret about the way that you treated them? Make the changes needed to live a life as free of regret as possible. Treat people with the same degree of respect

and appreciation that you desire. As the old saying goes, "Be careful how you treat people." You truly do reap what you sow, or in modern terms - Karma is a bitch.

19.   Be humble and don't be afraid to apologize. Some people have the idea that if they apologize to someone it will make them appear weak. On the contrary, it shows that you are strong, secure, and not prideful. It shows that you care about the offended party and their feelings. It shows that you have good character and it takes nothing away from your womanhood or manhood. It is very important in relationships. The Bible says not to let the sun go down while you are angry. Ephesians 4:26. Proverbs 15:1 says that a soft answer turns away anger. Good communication is very important in any relationship and you will have a much better one if you learn and utilize each other's love language. There is a great book called *The Five Love Languages* by Gary Chapman. I highly recommend it. In it, he states that there are five basic ways that each of us prefers to give and receive love. They are, Words of Affirmation, Acts of Service, Giving and Receiving Gifts, Quality Time, and Physical Touch. He says that discovering your and your partner's primary love language will help you to create a stronger bond in your relationship. This book

will be very helpful in understanding how to love your partner in the way that will bring you the best response.

20. Be kind to everyone you meet, even if you don't like them and can't allow them close to you. You can show them courtesy. Do your best to be especially kind to children and the elderly. These two segments of society are especially vulnerable to those who prey on other people's weaknesses. That is just plain sick! I will never understand how anyone can abuse or molest an innocent, helpless child. Or mistreat anyone, but especially a defenseless older person who is weak and frail. It amazes me when people don't help their parents when they grow old and sick and can't support themselves. I have heard it said that, how can one man and one woman care for and raise five children and when they are grown, those five children cannot get together and in turn care for those two parents. It is very true that there are no perfect parents. If they did not purposely abuse, molest, or neglect you but did their best to give you a good upbringing in a safe, healthy home, you should do your best to take care of them when they need it. It amazes me that people sit by and let people die, especially parents, then scream, holler, cry, and try to drag them out of their coffin at their funeral. That absolutely fascinates me.

21. Different people believe in different things, and that is their right. But one thing is certain. Tomorrow is not promised. I am a devout Christian. I whole-heartedly believe that Jesus is the Son of God who came to earth by virgin birth, suffered, and died on Calvary's cross, rose again on the third day, ascended into heaven and is seated at God the Father's right hand. And is coming again for a glorious church without a spot or a wrinkle. I believe in the Holy Spirit and that He is alive and dwells in me. Am I perfect? By no means am I perfect. But I am saved. God is not looking for perfection. Legalism and the spirit of the Pharisee says that you must be perfect and obey all the laws to get into heaven. The simple yet profound truth is that salvation according to the Bible is found in Romans 10:9-10. Believe in your heart that Jesus is the Son of God and confess with your mouth that God raised him from the dead, and you shall be saved. Simple. The profound part is that your belief and confession must be genuine. It is not simply a matter of repeating the words. You truly must believe them and have faith in God. All of Christianity hinges on real, childlike faith. Salvation is such an awesome, overwhelming concept. It is mind-blowing to think as John 3:16 says that "God loved this sinful world so much that He gave His only Son to die as a sacrifice that we may have access not only to heaven and

everlasting life but also to a taste of heaven here on earth." He died to give us abundant life. Don't ever let the devil or anyone tell you that God doesn't love you. Even at your worst, God loves you. He loves the most horrible person on earth and died for them. I hate to hear people say that God doesn't love gay people. There are no exclusions in the map to salvation. God loves us he simply does not love everything we do. That goes for gay and straight people. I recommend that you accept Him as your Savior and ask Him to help you live your life and achieve your goals and have abundant life. Not everyone will be rich but you can have a happy, joyful, love-filled, blessed life. Money won't make you happy. Many rich people are miserable. They simply dress better, drive better, and live better while they are miserable. Look at Robin Williams and all the other celebrities and rich people who commit suicide. Live your life by faith. Faith is the currency which allows you to transact spiritual business. God is a spirit and those who worship Him must do it in spirit and in truth. John 4:24. Hebrews 11 is called the Hall Of Faith. It chronicles the great things that were done by faith. Miracles happen by faith and God is still in the miracle-working business. Read and believe His word and trust Him like a child trusts a good father. Let your faith in God and His word profit you. Hebrews 4:2 says that God's word did not profit them because it was not mixed with faith. People go to church, read the Bible, and say prayers with no results. Why? Because they have no faith. Faith is currency, like money is currency. It will not simply get you what you want. Thank God! Because sometimes you want something that is not good for you and that God knows will harm you. Proverbs 37:4 says "delight yourself in the Lord and He will give you the desires of your heart". That does not mean that He gives you everything that you want. He will give you the desires of your heart because your heart is right before Him and your desires line up with His desires for you. 2 Corinthians 16:9 says that "the eyes of the Lord run to and fro throughout the whole earth searching for those whose heart is perfect(-mature) towards Him." 1 Samuel 16:7 says "man looks on the outward appearance, but God looks on the heart". Proverbs 4:23 says "guard your heart with all diligence for out of it flows the issues of life". Keep a pure heart. Don't let past hurts cause you to become bitter. Guard your heart. Matthew 22:37 says "love God with all your heart, soul, mind and strength. Let God's love wash away the pain from your soul. And love your neighbor as yourself. Not everyone loves themselves. Some people hate themselves. I used to be one of them. If you don't love yourself you will never be able to love others properly. Your vision is clouded. You think that no one will love you because of your self-image. You think of yourself as damaged goods. God doesn't see you that way and He doesn't want you to see yourself that way. This is the reason that many people are depressed and live with self-loathing. I was one of those people. But God! Whom the Son sets free is free indeed. I began to talk to myself in a positive way. I said to myself what God says about me as His child. I am the head, not the tail. I am above, not beneath. I will lend and not borrow. I am a joint-heir with Christ Jesus. I quoted and repeated this to myself over and over. God loves me. I am loveable. Over and over. Every time a negative thought came. I suffered from clinical depression so severe that there was a time that I truly wanted to die to escape the mental anguish and physical pain. I went to the doctor and began taking medicine to correct a chemical imbalance causing the depression. And with faith in God, therapy, and medicine, I am the most positive person I know. There is no shame in seeking help for a mental or physical condition. Medicine helps with symptoms, but Jesus is the only healer. Taking medicine doesn't diminish your faith. God works through medicine as well as miracles. Actually, the fact that the scientists found the right chemical combination to make the medicine is a miracle itself.

22. As you go through life it is important that you grow through life. Don't be a person who ages but doesn't mature. As they say, there is no fool like an old fool. Experience all the good things that life has to offer. Don't get involved in pettiness and things that you know you will regret later. Live each day to its fullest potential while being your best, most unique self. Never copy anyone, be yourself. God made each of us with special characteristics. Even identical twins are unique in their own way. No matter how you look, you are beautiful. Don't let the fact that you are not what the world or the media calls beautiful or attractive stop you from appreciating yourself and achieving your goals. Work hard and get your education. Do as Les Brown says and "shoot for the moon so even if you miss you will land among the stars." This is the only life you have. One shot. Make the most of it and do your best. As the song by Lil Duval and Snoop Dogg says, "I'm living my best life; I ain't going back and forth with you." Be mature, respectable, and responsible. Carry yourself in a friendly, no-nonsense way and avoid foolishness and immaturity. Don't argue with people. Silly, petty things need not be acknowledged. Rise above it and stay above it. Be the bigger, better person. Respect yourself and keep a great appreciation for this one life that God has

blessed you with. Other people will respect you also whether they like you or admit to it.

23. Be a trailblazer. Take the time to venture out both literally and figuratively. Explore new things and discover your natural gifts and talents. Do as much self-exploration and self-discovery as possible. Once you discover your gifts and the things that you enjoy, find out if you can turn them into a marketable business. I am an entrepreneur at heart. I love being my own boss. Even with all the pressures and responsibilities that go with it, I love it. I started my first business in my early twenties. It doesn't always cost a lot of money to start-up. At present, I work for someone else. But I am planning to and working towards opening several other businesses. Being my own boss is very satisfying to me and if I do that and work for someone else, it creates dual or multiple incomes. There is great joy and satisfaction in doing what you love and getting paid for it. You will not believe that you are getting paid for doing it because it doesn't feel like you are working. You are simply doing what you love and enjoy.

24. I am a caregiver by nature and have worked many years in the medical field as a caregiver with the elderly. Even as a child I spent most of my time with an elderly widow

named Ms. Ruby. We loved each other and had a grand-mother/granddaughter relationship. She passed away suddenly at the age of 82 when I was 12. I was devastated. She was the first person that I was really close to, that died. I realize now that as much of a shock to me as her death was, it was a blessing not to have to watch her suffer. I loved her dearly. Whether you are a natural caregiver or not, you may be, at some point in your life, thrust into the caregiving role with a sick loved-one. It may be a child or grandchild who needs full or part-time care. Or it may be an adult, whether elderly or not who becomes sick and needs caring for. Many times the bulk of the responsibility falls on one particular family member and this may wear that person out. If the entire family will band together to assist in the care of sick loved-ones, it will be much less stressful. Someone can help bathe, another can grocery shop, another can sit and talk with or play a game with the person, and it won't be so overwhelming. Alzheimer's and dementia are very common illnesses among the elderly today. It is important to take the time and do some research about these illnesses and their causes and symptoms so that you can recognize the warning signs. This will help you to better relate to that person. Those affected by these diseases may have to be placed in a nursing facility to be watched and cared for at some point. But please don't forget about and abandon them. I have worked in these types of facilities, and it is heart-breaking to hear the residents there talk about how lonely they are and the fact that their family members do not come to see them and make sure that they receive the proper care. Even if they don't remember everything and at some point, they may not recognize you anymore, but still go visit. Take them their favorite meal or candy or a flower. Little things mean so much when you have so little and are alone. Many times even those with dementia or Alzheimer's have occasions when they are lucid and are in the proper state of mind and when they realize how their life has shrunk and that they are confined to the facility, they cry uncontrollably. My grandmother had these conditions and although I visited her regularly she did not remember and constantly asked for me. My grandmother was a very smart, strong woman and it hurt deeply to see her in that condition but I always remembered how she was there for me when I needed her throughout the years, and I made a point of going to see her and doing things to brighten her day. Now that she is gone, I have no regrets about the way I treated her. You cannot take an "out of sight, out of mind" attitude when it comes to your sick loved ones. They need you. Not acknowledging the hard issues that you face in life does not make them go away. They must be dealt with. This "look the other way and pretend I don't see" attitude is how abuse and molestations continue. Life is not always easy. There are hard, ugly things that must be dealt with and addressed in order to stop them. While seeing her hurt like that, I always remembered that she was *my* grandmother. A woman who loved me and would do anything for me and any of her other family members. I would never abandon her when she needed me simply because it made me uncomfortable. I put my "big girl" panties on and dealt with the situation responsibly. Now that she's gone I am so glad that I did. I live by the philosophy that I give flowers to the living, not to the dead. While you are alive you can both enjoy them. Love and appreciate people while they are here with you. Show them and tell them how you feel. Live a life so that you don't have a lot of unnecessary regret… Selah (meditate on this).

25. Men- make sure that you provide for your families. That includes the children that you helped to create who live with you and those who don't. Your older children do not deserve to be neglected simply because you decided to go off and create a whole new group of children and family. They did not ask to come here. If you don't want to be a father and support your own children, I suggest you strap-up because these children are not going

anywhere, and neither is Maury Povich and DNA testing. You are the father! Act like it! Selah (meditate on this). But providing is only the beginning. A woman needs to know that you love, respect, and appreciate her and that you would take a bullet to protect her, if necessary. Be a gentleman with a lion's nature. Make sure that she is secure in your relationship. Let her know that you are with her and for her and that you want to be there. Tell her and show her that she is beautiful and special and that of all the women that you have met, you know that she is the one for you. Tell her that you chose her and continue to choose her all day, every day. Cover her with your arms, love, and prayers. If you do that and touch her gently in non-sexual ways, you won't have any trouble getting sex from her. No man is sexier than one who works hard, bringing home a paycheck for his family (large or small paycheck). Playing with his kids and helping them with their homework, loading and unloading the dishwasher, and folding clothes. That, truly is, the sexiest man alive and a true turn-on. If she chose to be with you and can trust and respect you, it won't matter if you are six foot five or five foot six. Height and weight have never made any man a "Big Man." Your ignorance and arrogance will surely show and be a real turn-off no matter how much money you make or how you over-compensate. While good sex is important, it is about so much more than penis-size. A good, respectful, honest, loving relationship is priceless. Build that kind of union and respect and preserve it. Most people never experience that kind of true-life love affair. If you find someone that you want to be with, work through the issues that are not deal-breakers and build something beautiful that will last a life-time. Remove cheating, lying, and dis-respect as options. Don't start with sex. Start with good communication and simply enjoy being with each other. Let love blossom. It will truly be worth it.

26. To the women. Be a woman who is strong, loving, kind, and trustworthy. Women say that a good man is hard to find. But the men say that a good woman is hard to find. Many men have a reputation for being scandalous. But unfortunately, so do many women. Many women are so desperate for a man and a husband that they have no problem going after yours, which has started the most ridiculous competition between women that I have ever seen. And it is sparked by some trifling imma-ture men who want their ego fed at your expense. I call men's ego the Beast! Do you not realize that any man (and I use the word loosely) who would do that to you is not worth your time? He has absolutely no respect for either of you. You can't trust him because as surely

as he fools you into thinking that you won, he will be sneaking behind your back with her and any other woman he can get. Making you both look like boo-boo the fool. He will never respect you and you will lose respect for yourself. Is he really worth that much to you? If so, why? It is a known fact that boys mature more slowly than girls and there will always be issues to work through. But don't let your desperation and your clock-ticking cause you to be foolish. Make these men treat you with respect. Be a mature woman in progress until you reach full maturity. Have respect for yourself, as well as for other women, and teach your daughters to do the same. Teach them to compete with themselves to become the best person they can be and not dis-re-spect themselves and each other by crossing lines. Understand that if he will cheat *with* you, he will cheat *on* you. Don't believe his lies about how much better you are than she is. If he talks bad about her to you, he will talk bad about you to the next woman. Recognize the game he's playing. They say, "bros before hoes" and they mean it. So, where is the sisterhood amongst women? I am so tired of seeing this repeated over and over. When will women learn? Carry yourself respect-ably and if he doesn't respect you, let him go! What have you lost? A man will never treat you better than you treat yourself, or than he treats his mother. Watch how he speaks to and treats the women in his life. No one is perfect but he should be a good-hearted person, who doesn't get enjoyment from mistreating and disrespecting people. Especially people who are weaker. If that is how he validates himself and feeds his ego, he is sick. Some people enjoy *praying for* people and some people enjoy *preying on* people. They are like vultures circling or sharks looking for the first sign of weakness or the smell of blood. Run girl, run! Run like Forrest Gump in the other direction and don't look back. He will destroy your life. George Gershwin wrote a song many years ago called "Someone to Watch Over Me." That's what a truly good man will do. He will care about you, care for you, and protect you. He will never feed his ego at your expense. Watch for those that you see prey on others. They will do the same to you and your children as soon as they get the chance. Love with your eyes open. Don't fool yourself. Don't say he will change. It is his discussion to see the need for change and to do the work to bring about that change. How much of your life are you willing to invest while waiting for him to change? Time is the one thing you can't get back. There are many miserable wives who got married with the mistaken idea that he will change. He must want to change. You need to address the big issues before you get tied down to him. Weddings may be expensive but divorces are too.

If you want to be with him and he needs counseling, encourage it and go with him in support if possible. Find someone worth investing your time and energy with. No one is perfect but he must be willing to help himself. If he won't work or doesn't support the children he already has, for the love of all that makes sense don't get pregnant! Don't fool yourself into thinking that you and your kids will somehow be so special that he will suddenly become responsible. People change because they want to change. Because they see the need to change, not for you. No man is perfect. A decent man that you like and treats you well is worth working with. But these vicious, self-absorbed men that my Grandma Gladys called "pairs of britches", they will suck the life out of you and destroy you. It won't matter if you live in a nice house with a nice car and money in the bank. They will destroy all that's good in you if you let them. Run girl, run!

27. Be beautiful, no matter how you look or what your age. Endeavor to be a beautiful person on the inside and let that beauty shine through. I am a 53 year old grand-mother of three and proud of it. I have a great sense of humor and am still very young at heart. Although I don't look like I did when I was young and am carrying some extra weight, I don't let it get me down. I am

working on losing the weight for the sake of my health and because I want to look better to myself. I know that I have a good heart and am, what we here in the south call, "good people". I do my best to look, smell, and dress as good as I can. I get my hair, nails, and feet done. You may not be able to afford those things right now but keep yourself and neat and clean as you can. Look and be your best. When people look at me, I hope that they look beyond the outer, superficial things and see my heart. I do my best to be and speak positively. I am an encourager and an exhorter. My heart's desire is for everyone to have their best possible life and reach their full potential. I want people to take charge of their lives and stop allowing negative things happen to them and their families. Some of these things are within our control and we are passive and allow them to happen, then complain about how much we hate them. Stop complaining and do what is necessary to help yourself and fix your life. This is your only chance at life. Do all you can to make it the most positive and best experience. Pray to God to lead you in everything. Handle what is within your control and pray even more about what is not. Remember the Serenity Prayer. "Lord help me to accept the things I cannot change. Help me change the things I can. And give me the wisdom to know the difference." Take control and live a beautiful life. It is up to you.

28. A good education is so important. Not everyone sees the value of a college education. Neither did I until later in life. I was 50 years old when I formally began college. After beginning a degree program, I decided to change to a certificate program and received my Human Resource certificate from the University of Phoenix. It is important to begin to teach small children at an early age. Music is a very valuable tool in teaching children of any age but especially in their formative years. That's why we learn to sing our ABCs before we say them. In reality, children are capable of learning so much more than that in their early years. Their little minds are like sponges absorbing everything around them. That's why you shouldn't say or do certain things in front of them or they will repeat them. Play games with them and figure out what their primary learning style is because not everyone learns in the same way or at the same pace. Some teachers teach classes by using only one teaching style and that is why some students do well and some do poorly in class. Your children will learn a lot more if you teach them according to their individual learning style. It is not the sole responsibility of the daycare, preschool, or any other school to educate your children.

My daughter was reading at 4 years because I took the time to teach her. And yes, I was a single mom with a full-time job at the time. Be a positive role-model and take advantage of the many teaching opportunities there are throughout the day to give them a life lesson as well as a book lesson. Give them visual (sight), audio (sound), taste, smell and hands-on lessons throughout the day. There are so many opportunities to teach. We have to give our children as good a head start as possible in this world. American students have lagged far behind students from other countries for many years even though we are a blessed country. Our priorities are out of order. Many people want to have babies but don't recognize the responsibility of being a good parent. Children are very important. They are our legacy. They are the ones who will shape the future. As the old saying goes "the hand that rocks the cradle, shapes the world." Give your children a safe, loving home and nurture them. Let them explore new things and find out what they like and do well at and help to develop them in those things. Celebrities like Tiger Woods and Venus and Serena Williams had parents who helped to nurture and encourage them and develop their gifts. And just look what happened to them.

29. The other day me and my mom (Clara) who had gotten sick and passed away in past years and how many of them have died without life insurance or burial insurance. This is a very common practice among people today and it leaves the spouses and children left behind in quite a bad predicament if there is not any money for the funeral, burial, or cremation. As I told her, I don't understand this way of thinking that it is someone else's responsibility to take care of your final expenses. As surely as you wake up in the morning, you must recognize that there is going to come a morning when you will not wake up. If you do not prepare for this day, you will leave your family members in a position to have to beg and borrow from whomever they can or try to negotiate with the funeral directors to take care of what you had years to take care of yourself. Don't leave your loved ones grieving your loss and under the stress of trying to figure out how to put you away. Take responsibility for your final arrangements. That day is surely coming. Selah (meditate on this).

30. It is not easy to blend a family. You and your children have your own routine, beliefs, and way of doing things and so does your partner and their family. To bring someone or more than one person into your inner circle will take some planning and work. Have a discussion

with each other, then with the entire family as to how things will change and how you plan to make this work before you make the decision to live together. Then get rid of the idea that your spouse's children are "step" children. If you can't love them and treat them as your own, perhaps you should think twice about this union. Your children will always be your children. They aren't going anywhere until one of you dies. Why would you bring someone into their home who mistreats or disrespects them? They did not ask to come here. You brought them here so take care of them and protect them.

31. One of the greatest problems that our society faces today is the lack of men with any degree of maturity. And the real problem is that these immature men have no problem procreating and being absentee fathers to a new generation of immature men. They run around having unprotected sex with different women and fooling themselves into thinking that these women won't get pregnant or that they can somehow dodge child support. They have no intention of taking care of the women they sleep with or the children they create. In fact, they have already made up their minds to deny the child from the first moment the women tell them that they are pregnant. They have no plans to offer any

financial or emotional support to these women and children. Some are so sorry that they not only don't support these children, but they don't even care if they never lay eyes on their own children. If you don't want a child, then use the head on your neck and use protection! This can be avoided by being responsible. Don't be a sperm donor who drops off his sperm and walks away as if he has no responsibility. A good father loves, cares for, supports, and protects his children. No one should have to force you to pay child support. If you eat, wear clothes, and have a place to sleep then your children need the same. All of them! If you don't want that responsibility for the next 18 years, then have responsible sex. The heat of the moment and those 5 or 10 seconds of ecstasy can have life-long repercussions. Is it really worth it? No one has to force a good man to take care of his children .He recognizes that it is his duty as a man to care for the children he brought here. He takes pride in it. There are millions of confused children, especially boys, who have serious abandonment issues because they don't have a healthy relationship with their fathers. Girls and boys looking for love in all the wrong places because of irresponsible parents. Decide to be an example to your children before you bring them into this world. The world is a scary place without a strong foundation and a good support network. That is why there are so many teen pregnancies and confused young people. So many young people are wandering through life looking for someone or something to bring them fulfillment because of the void left by absentee fathers. So many are being bullied at school and taking their own lives because they have no roots or a strong family network. All they want to do is get rich because they think that they will finally be happy and fulfilled. That is a gross misconception. Riches won't make you happy. Knowing who you are and being secure in who you are makes the difference. The break-down of the family has all but destroyed our society. Women are struggling to raise children as single parents. As good as we are as women there is only so much that we can teach our sons about being a man. But these men are so lost themselves that they are not only not there for the children, but have no idea what to teach their sons if they do spend time with them. It is also very important to girls to have a healthy relationship with their fathers. The fact that they don't is the reason that they are chasing these boys at such an early age. I hate to think of the damage these immature men who absolutely refuse to grow up have caused to society. We really do need the men to stand up and *be* men! It is important! You are supposed to be the leader and the head of the family. Can you honestly say that you have done that? You want the honor and respect that goes with the role but are you fulfilling the responsibilities that the role entails? Find your sufficiency and completeness in Jesus Christ and let Him help you and bless you to live and gain the life he has for you. Abundant life that brings you the joy that only comes from God. I want to see men stand up and be men and stop playing childish games. There are lives at stake, mainly your own children's lives. And the same goes for women. There is hope that we can turn this generation around if we stop making excuses for ourselves and begin to stand up and be counted as strong mature men and women who want better for future generations. Take a stand for yourself and your family. Together we can make a real difference in this world. Selah (meditate on this).